Young Goodman Brown

A Dark Allegory of Faith, Temptation
& the Evil That Lurks in Every Soul

A Modern Translation
Adapted for the Contemporary Reader

Nathaniel Hawthorne

Translated by Tim Zengerink

Table of Contents

Preface
Message to the Reader

Rebuilding the Greatest Library in Human History

Thousands of years ago, the Library of Alexandria was the heart of global knowledge — a sanctuary where the wisdom of every known civilization was gathered and shared freely.

And then, it was lost.

Now, we're rebuilding it — and you are invited to join us.

At the Library of Alexandria, we've set out to make every book available to every person on Earth — not just in print, but in every language, every format, and for every reader.

Here's how we do it:

- **Deluxe Print Editions at True Printing Cost** - Order any book as a high-quality paperback, elegant hardcover, or stunning boxset — and only pay what it costs to print. No markups. No middlemen.
- **Unlimited Access to the Greatest Works** - Enjoy thousands of timeless classics — from Plato to Shakespeare to Tolstoy — in beautiful, modern eBook and audiobook editions. Read and listen without limits — for every reader, everywhere.
- **Modern Translations for Every Language & Dialect** - We're reimagining the classics in clear, accessible language — and translating them into every dialect imaginable. Everyone deserves to understand humanity's greatest ideas.

When you visit **LibraryofAlexandria.com**, you're not just accessing books — you're joining a global movement to restore, preserve, and share the wisdom of civilization.

Join us today at LibraryofAlexandria.com

Together, we'll ensure the light of human wisdom never fades again.

With gratitude,

The Modern Library of Alexandria Team

Visit:
www.libraryofalexandria.com
Or scan the code below:

Introduction

Into the Forest of the Soul: The Journey from Innocence to Dread

Nathaniel Hawthorne's *Young Goodman Brown* is one of the most haunting and provocative short stories in American literature—a compact yet profoundly disturbing allegory about the loss of innocence, the fragility of faith, and the universal potential for evil within the human heart. First published in 1835, the tale continues to resonate because it taps into some of the deepest anxieties of human existence: the fear of hypocrisy, the lure of temptation, and the suspicion that even the most upright people carry darkness within them.

Set in 17th-century Puritan New England—a world already rich in moral absolutism, religious rigidity, and suspicion—the story follows Goodman Brown, a young man who leaves his wife Faith behind one night to venture into the forest. Ostensibly on an unnamed "errand," Brown quickly finds himself on a surreal and increasingly diabolical journey that undermines everything he thought he knew about morality, community, and himself. What he witnesses (or believes he witnesses) in the woods—a gathering of seemingly all the pious and upright citizens of his town participating in a satanic ritual—shatters his trust in human goodness.

This brief narrative is layered with meaning, ambiguity, and symbolism, and Hawthorne intentionally refuses to make clear whether Brown's experiences are literal, psychological, or supernatural. That ambiguity is precisely the point. The story is not just about what happens in the woods, but about what happens to Brown's perception of the world—and what that says about the Puritan mindset, the American psyche, and the human condition.

Hawthorne's writing is rooted in his own legacy: he was the descendant of John Hathorne, a judge in the Salem witch trials, and much of his fiction grapples with the burden of inherited guilt, religious repression, and moral scrutiny. *Young Goodman Brown* functions as both a historical allegory and a timeless parable. Though grounded in a specific time and place, its themes are eternal. What happens when one begins to doubt the sincerity of those around them? What happens when one glimpses the evil that might lurk behind every virtuous facade? Can one ever go back to believing in goodness, once one has looked into the abyss?

Brown's journey into the woods is, above all, a journey into himself. The forest, in literature and myth, has long been a symbol of mystery, danger, and transformation. In Young Goodman Brown, it becomes a psychological labyrinth—dark, tangled, and filled with whispers. As he ventures deeper, Brown loses not only his direction but his grip on what is real, what is right, and who he truly is. And when he returns to his village the next morning, he is forever changed—estranged from his wife, alienated from his community, and consumed by suspicion and sorrow.

Allegory, Symbolism, and the Collapse of Moral Certainty

Young Goodman Brown is rich with allegorical significance. Nearly every character, setting, and object functions on multiple levels, contributing to the story's psychological depth and thematic complexity. The protagonist's name,

"Goodman Brown," is no accident. "Goodman" was a common title for Puritan men, suggesting everyman status, while "Brown" is an earthy, humble surname. Together, they signify an ordinary individual—a man meant to stand in for all of us—who undergoes an extraordinary crisis of faith.

Likewise, the name of his wife—Faith—is both literal and symbolic. She is described with pink ribbons in her hair, an image of innocence and purity. When Brown leaves her behind, it is not just a marital parting—it represents a spiritual decision to depart from trust and belief. Throughout the story, her voice echoes in his mind as a symbol of moral grounding, and when he thinks she has succumbed to evil in the forest ritual, it marks the emotional and spiritual climax of his collapse.

The forest itself is not just a setting; it is a manifestation of the unknown, the subconscious, and the morally ambiguous. In contrast to the structured world of the Puritan village—with its rules, sermons, and visible order— the forest is where chaos reigns, identities blur, and truth dissolves. It is here that Brown meets a mysterious man with a serpent-like staff—clearly an allusion to the Devil or a satanic figure. This man knows Brown's ancestors, recounts their sins, and reveals the dark complicity of Brown's lineage in acts of violence and persecution. This dialogue suggests that evil is not foreign to Brown—it is part of his heritage.

As Brown journeys deeper, he sees more and more respected members of his town—ministers, deacons, pious women—making their way to a black mass. Whether this event actually occurs or is a hallucination caused by guilt, fear, or dream logic is deliberately unclear. But the effect is the same: Brown loses the ability to believe in anyone's virtue. When he returns to town and sees the same people in the light of day, he cannot unsee the darkness he believes he has witnessed. His spiritual paranoia renders him emotionally and socially dead. He lives out his days in gloom, "his dying hour was gloom," Hawthorne writes.

At its heart, Young Goodman Brown is about the destruction of idealism. Brown wants to believe in the purity of others—and of himself. But the forest teaches him that evil is universal, that no one is above temptation or corruption. This revelation, rather than liberating him, ruins him. It creates a kind of moral nihilism. Unable to trust, he retreats into isolation and judgment. Hawthorne thus warns against both blind faith and crippling cynicism. The human soul, he suggests, is always in tension between virtue and vice. The danger lies not in recognizing evil, but in letting the recognition destroy all possibility of goodness.

Historical Roots, Lasting Impact, and the American Moral Landscape

To fully appreciate *Young Goodman Brown*, it is helpful to place it within its historical and literary context. Hawthorne was writing during the American Romantic period, a time when writers like Poe, Melville, and Emerson were exploring individualism, nature, spirituality, and the darker aspects of the self. But Hawthorne's unique focus was on the moral and psychological legacy of Puritanism. His stories often revolve around sin, secrecy, repression, and the devastating consequences of moral absolutism.

Hawthorne himself was deeply conflicted about his Puritan ancestry. He changed the spelling of his family name to distance himself from his ancestor's role in the witch trials, but the weight of that heritage permeates his work. In *Young Goodman Brown*, this burden takes the form of historical continuity: the idea that the sins of the past live on in the present, shaping who we are whether we acknowledge them or not.

The Salem witch trials, a backdrop to the story, symbolize a society that claims to seek righteousness but becomes consumed by fear, hysteria, and persecution. Hawthorne's critique is subtle but powerful: he exposes the danger of a society obsessed with sin but blind to compassion. In Goodman Brown's transformation, we see the spiritual damage that results when one prioritizes judgment over empathy, appearance over substance, and certainty over grace.

Since its publication, the story has become a staple of American literature, studied for its allegorical structure, psychological insight, and theological implications. Its themes have echoed through countless works of fiction, from modern horror and gothic tales to explorations of religious trauma and social hypocrisy. Writers such as Flannery O'Connor, Shirley Jackson, and even Stephen King have inherited Hawthorne's interest in the thin veil between good and evil, sanity and delusion, faith and fear.

In contemporary times, *Young Goodman Brown* remains relevant because it captures a universal and enduring truth: the human soul is complex, and the world is rarely black and white. We all carry contradictions. We all wrestle with doubt, pride, and temptation. And we all must decide whether to look for the good in others—or be consumed by their flaws.

Hawthorne's story does not end with hope—but it does end with clarity. Brown's journey into the forest reveals not just the evil that others may harbor, but the fear and judgment within himself. That self-knowledge, though painful, is perhaps the most honest part of the story.

To read *Young Goodman Brown* is to take a walk into your own forest of doubt. It challenges you to question what you believe about others, and about yourself. It warns against both naivety and despair. And like all great allegories, it never stops asking questions. What do you see when you look into the heart of the woods? And when you return, will you ever be the same?

Chapter 1

Young Goodman Brown stepped out into the street of Salem village as the sun was setting. After crossing the threshold, he turned back to share a farewell kiss with his young wife. Faith, whose name perfectly suited her, leaned her lovely head out into the street, allowing the wind to toy with the pink ribbons on her cap as she called out to Goodman Brown.

"My dearest love," she whispered softly and with a touch of sadness, her lips close to his ear, "please postpone your journey until sunrise and sleep in your own bed tonight. A woman alone is troubled by such dreams and such thoughts that she sometimes fears herself. Please stay with me this night, dear husband, of all nights in the year."

"My love and my Faith," replied young Goodman Brown, "of all nights in the year, I must stay away from you this one night. My journey, as you call it, there and back again, must be completed between now and sunrise. What, my sweet, pretty wife, do you doubt me already, and we've only been married three months?"

"Then God bless you!" said Faith, with the pink ribbons; "and may you find all well when you come back."

"Amen!" cried Goodman Brown. "Say your prayers, dear Faith, and go to bed at dusk, and no harm will come to you."

So they said goodbye; and the young man continued on his path until, as he was about to turn the corner by the meeting-house, he glanced back and saw Faith's head still watching him with a sad expression, despite her pink ribbons.

"Poor little Faith!" he thought, as his heart filled with guilt. "What a terrible person I am to leave her for such a task! She mentioned dreams, too. I thought as she spoke that there was worry in her face, as if a dream had warned her about what work needs to be done tonight. But no, no; it would kill her to think about it. Well, she's a blessed angel on earth; and after this one night I'll hold onto her and follow her to heaven."

With this excellent plan for the future, Goodman Brown felt he had good reason to hurry toward his current wicked goal. He had chosen a gloomy road, made dark by the most forbidding trees in the forest, which barely moved aside to allow the narrow path to wind through before closing in again immediately. The place was as isolated as anywhere could be; and there's something unique about this kind of isolation—the traveler never knows who might be hidden among the countless tree trunks and thick branches above, so that even while walking alone, he might actually be moving through an invisible crowd.

"There might be a dangerous Indian hiding behind every tree," Goodman Brown said to himself, and he looked nervously over his shoulder as he continued, "What if the devil himself is standing right next to me!"

With his head turned back, he rounded a bend in the road, and when he looked forward again, he saw a man dressed in serious and respectable clothing, sitting at the base of an old tree. The man stood up as Goodman Brown approached and began walking alongside him.

"You're late, Goodman Brown," he said. "The clock at Old South was chiming when I passed through Boston, and that was a full fifteen minutes ago."

"Faith held me back for a moment," the young man replied, his voice trembling from his companion's sudden appearance, though he hadn't been completely caught off guard.

It was now deep twilight in the forest, and darkest in that section where these two men were traveling. As far as anyone could tell, the second traveler appeared to be around fifty years old, seemingly from the same social class as Goodman Brown, and sharing a striking resemblance to him, though perhaps more in facial expression than in actual features. They could easily have been mistaken for father and son. Yet, while the older man was dressed as plainly as the younger one, and carried himself with equal simplicity, he possessed an unmistakable quality of someone who understood the world, someone who wouldn't have felt uncomfortable at the governor's dinner table or in King William's court, if circumstances had ever brought him to such places. However, the only aspect of his appearance that stood out as truly noteworthy was his walking stick, which resembled a large black snake, crafted so skillfully that it almost seemed to twist and writhe like a living serpent. This effect, naturally, must have been a trick of the eye, enhanced by the dim and shifting light.

"Come on, Goodman Brown," called out his traveling companion, "this is a slow pace for starting a journey. Take my walking stick if you're already getting tired."

"Friend," said the other, stopping completely after his slow walk, "since I've kept my promise by meeting you here, I now intend to return where I came from. I have moral concerns about the matter you know of."

"Is that what you say?" he replied with the serpent, smiling to himself. "Let's keep walking anyway and talk as we go. If I don't convince you, then you can turn back. We've only gone a short way into the forest so far."

"Too far! Too far!" the good man cried out, without realizing he had started walking again. "My father never ventured into these woods for such a purpose, nor did his father before him. We've been a family of honest men and good Christians since the time of the martyrs, and am I to be the first Brown to ever take this path and keep—"

"You're thinking about the kind of company you'd be keeping," the older man said, reading the meaning behind his hesitation. "Well put, Goodman Brown! I've known your family as well as any among the Puritans, and that's saying quite a lot. I assisted your grandfather, the constable, when he whipped that Quaker woman so thoroughly through Salem's streets; and I was the one who gave your father a burning pine torch, lit from my own fireplace, to burn down an Indian village during King Philip's War. Both were dear friends of mine; we took many enjoyable walks along this very path and came back in good spirits well past midnight. I'd be happy to befriend you for their memory."

"If what you're saying is true," Goodman Brown replied, "I'm amazed they never mentioned these things. Actually, on second thought, maybe I'm not so surprised, since even the smallest whisper of such behavior would have gotten them kicked out of New England. We're people who believe in prayer and doing good deeds, and we don't tolerate that kind of evil."

"Whether it's wickedness or not," said the traveler carrying the twisted staff, "I'm well-connected throughout New England. Church deacons from many congregations have shared communion wine with me; town selectmen from various communities have made me their leader; and most members of the Great and General Court strongly support my cause. The governor and I also—but those are matters of state secrecy."

"Can this really be true?" cried Goodman Brown, staring in amazement at his calm companion. "However, I have nothing to do with the governor and council; they have their own ways, and they're no example for a simple farmer like me. But if I were to continue with you, how could I look that good old man, our minister at Salem village, in the eye? Oh, his voice would make me tremble both on Sunday and during his sermons."

Up to this point, the older traveler had listened with appropriate seriousness; but now he exploded into uncontrollable laughter, shaking himself so forcefully that his serpent-like walking stick appeared to writhe along with him.

"Ha! ha! ha!" he shouted over and over again; then pulling himself together, "Well, go on, Goodman Brown, go on; but please, don't kill me with laughter."

"Well then, to settle this once and for all," said Goodman Brown, clearly irritated, "there's my wife, Faith. It would shatter her sweet little heart, and I'd rather shatter my own instead."

"No, if that's the situation," replied the other, "then go on your way, Goodman Brown. I wouldn't want Faith to come to any harm for the sake of twenty old women like the one hobbling ahead of us."

As he spoke, he pointed his staff toward a woman on the path, and Goodman Brown recognized her as an extremely devout and virtuous lady who had taught him his catechism when he was young and continued to serve as his moral and spiritual guide alongside the minister and Deacon Gookin.

"It's truly amazing that Goody Cloyse would be so deep in the wilderness at nightfall," he said. "But if you don't mind, friend, I'll take a shortcut through the woods until we've left this Christian woman behind. Since she doesn't know you, she might ask who I was traveling with and where I was headed."

"So be it," said his traveling companion. "Go into the woods, and let me stay on the path."

The young man stepped aside but made sure to keep an eye on his companion, who moved quietly down the road until he was within striking distance of the elderly woman. She, in the meantime, was hurrying along as fast as she could—remarkably quick for someone her age—muttering unclear words under her breath, probably a prayer, as she walked. The traveler extended his staff and touched her wrinkled neck with what appeared to be the serpent's tail.

"The devil!" screamed the pious old lady.

"Then Goody Cloyse recognizes her old friend?" the traveler remarked, facing her while leaning on his twisting staff.

"Oh my goodness, is it really you, your worship?" exclaimed the good woman. "Yes, it truly is, and you look exactly like my old friend, Goodman Brown, the grandfather of that foolish fellow who lives now. But— would your worship believe it?—my broomstick has mysteriously vanished, stolen, I suspect, by that witch who hasn't been hanged yet, Goody Cory, and this happened right when I had covered myself with the juice of wild celery, cinquefoil, and wolfsbane."

"Mixed with fine wheat and the fat of a newborn baby," said the figure of old Goodman Brown.

"Oh, you know the secret," exclaimed the elderly woman, laughing loudly. "So, as I was explaining, being completely prepared for the gathering, and having no horse to ride, I decided to walk there on foot; for I've been told there's a pleasant young man who will be welcomed into our fellowship tonight. But now your honor will offer me your arm, and we'll arrive there in no time."

"That's hardly possible," her friend replied. "I can't offer you my arm, Goody Cloyse, but here's my staff if you'd like it."

After saying this, he threw it down at her feet, where it might have come to life, since it was one of the rods that its owner had previously given to the Egyptian magicians. Goodman Brown couldn't witness this happening, though. He had looked up in shock, and when he glanced down again, he saw neither Goody Cloyse nor the snake-like staff, but only his traveling companion, who waited for him as peacefully as if nothing had occurred.

"That elderly woman taught me my catechism," the young man said, and there was a wealth of meaning in this straightforward remark.

They kept walking forward, with the older traveler urging his companion to pick up the pace and stay on the path, speaking so persuasively that his words seemed to arise naturally from within his listener rather than being suggested from outside. As they walked, he broke off a maple branch to use as a walking stick and started removing the twigs and smaller branches, which were damp with evening dew. The instant his fingers made contact with them, they became remarkably withered and dried out, as if they had been exposed to a week of intense sunlight. The two men continued at a steady, brisk pace until suddenly, in a dark depression along the road, Goodman Brown sat down on a tree stump and refused to go any further.

"Friend," he said stubbornly, "I've made my decision. I won't take another step on this mission. What if some miserable old woman chooses to go to hell when I thought she was heading to heaven—is that any reason why I should abandon my dear Faith and follow her?"

"You'll change your mind about this eventually," his companion said calmly. "Sit here and rest for a while; and when you're ready to move again, you can use my walking stick to help you along."

Without another word, he tossed the maple stick to his companion and disappeared from view as quickly as if he had melted into the growing darkness. The young man remained by the roadside for a few moments, congratulating himself immensely and imagining how clear his conscience would be when he encountered the minister during his morning walk, and how he wouldn't need to avoid the gaze of good old Deacon Gookin. He thought about what peaceful sleep awaited him that very night, which had been intended for such wicked purposes but would now be spent so innocently and blissfully in Faith's embrace! While lost in these delightful and admirable thoughts, Goodman Brown heard the sound of horses' hooves approaching along the road and decided it would be wise to hide at the edge of the forest, aware of the sinful intention that had originally brought him to this place, even though he had now fortunately abandoned it.

The sound of hoofbeats and the voices of the riders approached, two serious old voices talking quietly as they came closer. These combined sounds seemed to travel along the road, just a few yards from where the young man was hiding; but because of the thick darkness in that particular spot, neither the travelers nor their horses could be seen. Even though their bodies brushed against the small branches beside the road, it was impossible to tell that they blocked, even briefly, the faint light from the strip of bright sky they must have crossed. Goodman Brown crouched down and stood on his toes by turns, pushing aside the branches and sticking his head out as far as he dared without being able to make out even a shadow. This frustrated him even more because he could have sworn, if such a thing were possible, that he recognized the voices of the minister and Deacon Gookin, riding along peacefully as they usually did when heading to some ordination or church council meeting. While still close enough to hear, one of the riders stopped to pick a small branch.

"Of the two, reverend sir," said the voice that sounded like the deacon's, "I would rather skip an ordination dinner than miss tonight's meeting. I've heard that some members of our community will be coming here from Falmouth and beyond, along with others from Connecticut and Rhode Island, plus several of the Indian medicine men who, in their own way, know nearly as much dark magic as the best of us. What's more, there's a virtuous young woman who will be brought into our fellowship."

"Excellent, Deacon Gookin!" the minister replied in his serious, aged voice. "Speed up, or we'll be late. You know nothing can be accomplished until I arrive there."

The hooves clattered once more, and the voices, speaking so eerily in the vacant air, continued on through the woods, where no church had ever been established or lone Christian had offered prayers. Where, then, could these devout men be traveling so far into the godless wilderness? Young Goodman Brown grasped a tree for stability, nearly collapsing to the earth, weak and overwhelmed by the profound anguish in his heart. He gazed upward at the sky, questioning whether heaven truly existed above him. Still, there was the blue dome overhead, with stars growing brighter within it.

"With heaven above and Faith below, I will yet stand firm against the devil!" cried Goodman Brown.

While he continued looking up into the deep curve of the sky with his hands raised in prayer, a cloud suddenly rushed across the highest point overhead and concealed the brightening stars, even though no wind was blowing. The blue sky remained visible everywhere except directly above, where this dark mass of cloud moved swiftly toward the north. High in the air, as though emerging from within the cloud itself, came a jumbled and uncertain sound of voices. At one point the listener thought he could make out the speech patterns of people from his own town, both men and women, some devout and others wicked, many of whom he had encountered at the communion table, while he had seen others causing disturbances at the tavern. The following moment, the sounds were so unclear that he questioned whether he had heard anything more than the murmuring of the ancient forest, rustling without any wind. Then a louder surge of those recognizable voices arose, sounds heard every day in the sunlight at Salem village, but never before this moment from a nighttime cloud. Among them was the voice of a young woman, crying out in distress, yet with a hesitant sadness, and pleading for some favor that might cause her pain to receive; and the entire invisible crowd, both holy and sinful people alike, appeared to be urging her forward.

"Faith!" Goodman Brown cried out, his voice filled with anguish and desperation; the forest echoes taunted him, calling back "Faith! Faith!" as though lost souls were searching for her throughout the entire wilderness.

The cry of grief, rage, and terror was still piercing through the night when the distraught husband held his breath, waiting for a response. There was a scream, immediately drowned out by a louder murmur of voices that faded into distant laughter as the dark cloud swept away, leaving the clear and silent sky above Goodman Brown. But something fluttered lightly down through the air and caught on the branch of a tree. The young man grabbed it and saw it was a pink ribbon.

"My faith is gone!" he cried out after a moment of stunned silence. "There is no good on earth, and sin is nothing but a word. Come, devil, for this world belongs to you."

Driven mad with despair, Goodman Brown laughed loudly and wildly as he grabbed his staff and started moving again, traveling so fast that he seemed to fly along the forest path rather than walk or run. The road became increasingly wild and desolate, growing fainter and fainter until it disappeared completely, leaving him deep in the heart of the dark wilderness, still rushing forward with the instinct that drives people toward evil. The entire forest was filled with terrifying sounds—the groaning of trees, the howling of wild animals, and the screams of Indians; sometimes the wind rang out like a distant church bell, and other times it roared all around the traveler, as if all of nature was mocking him. But he himself was the most frightening thing in the scene, and he didn't shrink away from any of the other horrors around him.

"Ha! ha! ha!" roared Goodman Brown when the wind laughed at him.

"Let's see who will have the last laugh. Don't think you can scare me with your evil tricks. Come on, witch, come on, wizard, come on, Indian medicine man, come on, devil himself—here comes Goodman Brown. You might as well be afraid of him as he is of you."

In reality, throughout the entire haunted forest there was nothing more terrifying than the sight of Goodman Brown. He rushed forward among the dark pine trees, waving his staff with wild movements, sometimes expressing terrible blasphemous thoughts, and other times bursting into such laughter that all the forest echoes seemed to laugh back like devils surrounding him. The devil in his true form is less frightening than when he burns with rage inside a human heart. This is how the possessed man raced along his path, until, trembling among the trees, he spotted a red glow ahead of him, like when fallen tree trunks and branches in a cleared area have been lit on fire, casting their eerie flames up against the night sky at midnight. He stopped during a brief calm in the storm that had pushed him forward, and heard what sounded like a hymn rising, rolling seriously from far away with the power of many voices. He recognized the melody; it was one he knew well from the choir of the village church. The verse faded away heavily, and was extended by a chorus made not of human voices, but of all the sounds of the dark wilderness joining together in terrible harmony. Goodman Brown shouted out, and his shout was lost to his own ears as it blended with the cry of the desert.

During the quiet moment, he crept forward until the bright light hit his face directly. At one end of a clearing, enclosed by the forest's dark walls, stood a large rock that looked somewhat like an altar or pulpit in its natural form. Four burning pine trees surrounded it, their tops engulfed in flames while their trunks remained untouched, resembling candles at an evening gathering. The thick vegetation covering the top of the rock was completely ablaze, sending flames high into the night sky and casting flickering light across the entire area. Every hanging branch and leafy decoration was on fire. As the red glow rose and dimmed, a large crowd appeared and vanished repeatedly in the shifting light and shadow, seeming to emerge from the darkness itself, filling the heart of the isolated woods all at once.

"A serious and darkly dressed group," said Goodman Brown.

In truth, that's exactly what they were. Among them, flickering back and forth between darkness and brightness, appeared faces that would be seen the next day at the provincial council meetings, and others who, Sunday after Sunday, gazed devoutly toward heaven and looked kindly over the packed church pews from the most sacred pulpits in the country. Some claim that the governor's wife was there. At the very least, there were prominent ladies well known to her, along with wives of respected husbands, widows in great numbers, elderly unmarried women of excellent reputation, and beautiful young women who trembled with fear that their mothers might spot them. Either the sudden flashes of light illuminating the dark field dazzled Goodman Brown, or he actually recognized about twenty church members from Salem village who were famous for their exceptional holiness. Good old Deacon Gookin had arrived and was waiting near that venerable saint, his respected pastor. But mixing inappropriately with these serious, respectable, and devout people—these church elders, these virtuous ladies and innocent young women—were men who lived immoral lives and women with tarnished reputations, people completely given over to every low and disgusting vice, and even suspected of terrible crimes. It was shocking to see that the good people didn't pull away from the evil ones, and the sinners weren't embarrassed in front of the saints. Scattered among their pale-faced enemies were also the Indian priests, or medicine men, who had often filled their native forests with more terrifying chants than anything known to English witchcraft.

"But where is Faith?" Goodman Brown wondered, and as hope filled his heart, he began to tremble.

Another verse of the hymn rose up, a slow and sorrowful melody that devout people would love, but it was set to words that expressed everything our human nature could imagine about sin, and darkly suggested even more. The knowledge of demons remains incomprehensible to ordinary mortals. Verse after verse was sung, and still the chorus from the wilderness swelled between them like the deepest sound of a massive organ. With the final crescendo of that terrible anthem came a sound, as if the roaring wind, the rushing streams, the howling beasts, and every other voice of the wild, untamed wilderness were blending and harmonizing with the voice of sinful humanity in worship to the prince of all evil. The four blazing pine trees threw up higher flames and dimly revealed shapes and faces of horror in the smoke clouds above the unholy gathering. At that same moment, the fire on the rock shot out red flames and formed a glowing arch above its base, where a figure now appeared. With respect be it said, the figure bore a strong resemblance, both in clothing and bearing, to some solemn minister of the New England churches.

"Bring forth the converts!" shouted a voice that rang across the field and carried into the forest.

At those words, Goodman Brown stepped out from the shadow of the trees and walked toward the gathering, feeling a disgusting kinship with them through the shared wickedness in his heart. He almost could have sworn that his own dead father's spirit was gesturing for him to come forward, looking down at him from a swirl of smoke, while a woman with the faint features of despair stretched out her hand to warn him away. Could it have been his mother? But he had no strength to step back even once, nor to resist, even in his thoughts, when the minister and good old Deacon Gookin grabbed his arms and guided him to the blazing rock. There also came the slim figure of a veiled woman, escorted between Goody Cloyse, that devout teacher of religious instruction, and Martha Carrier, who had been given the devil's promise to become queen of hell. She was a wild and vicious witch. And there the converts stood beneath the canopy of fire.

"Welcome, my children," said the dark figure, "to the communion of your race. You have discovered your true nature and your destiny at such a young age. My children, look behind you!"

They turned around, and suddenly appearing like a burst of fire, the devil worshippers could be seen; a dark welcoming smile glowed on every face.

"There," the dark figure continued, "are all the people you have looked up to since you were young. You thought they were more holy than you, and you pulled back from your own sins, comparing them to these people's righteous lives and their prayers reaching toward heaven. Yet here they all are in my congregation of worshippers. Tonight you will be allowed to learn about their hidden actions: how gray-bearded church elders have spoken lustful words to the young women in their homes; how many wives, eager to become widows, have given their husbands a drink before bed and let them sleep their final sleep in their arms; how young men without beards have hurried to inherit their fathers' money; and how beautiful young women—don't blush, sweet ones—have dug small graves in the garden, and invited me, the only guest to a baby's funeral. Through your human hearts' understanding of sin, you will be able to detect all the places—whether in church, bedroom, street, field, or forest—where crimes have been committed, and you will rejoice to see the whole earth as one stain of guilt, one enormous bloodstain. Much more than this. You will be able to see into every heart the deep mystery of sin, the source of all evil practices, and which endlessly provides more wicked urges than human power—than my power at its greatest—can reveal through actions. And now, my children, look at each other."

They followed the command; and in the flickering light of those hellish torches, the miserable man saw his Faith, while his wife saw her husband, both shaking with fear before that unholy altar.

"Look, there you stand, my children," said the figure, in a deep and solemn tone, almost sad with its despairing awfulness, as if his once angelic nature could still mourn for our miserable race. "Depending upon one another's hearts, you had still hoped that virtue was not all a dream. Now you are undeceived. Evil is the nature of mankind. Evil must be your only happiness. Welcome again, my children, to the communion of your race."

"Welcome," the devil worshippers repeated, their voices joining together in a single cry that mixed despair and triumph.

And there they stood, the only couple who seemed to still be wavering on the edge of evil in this dark world. A basin had been carved naturally into the rock. Did it hold water that appeared red in the eerie light? Or was it blood? Or perhaps some kind of liquid fire? The evil figure dipped his hand into this substance and prepared to mark their foreheads with a baptism that would make them participants in the mystery of sin, more aware of others' secret guilt in both actions and thoughts than they could ever be of their own wrongdoing. The husband glanced once at his pale wife, and Faith looked back at him. What corrupted beings would their next look reveal them to be to each other, both trembling at what they would expose and what they would witness!

"Faith! Faith!" shouted the husband, "look up to heaven, and resist the evil one."

Whether Faith obeyed, he didn't know. As soon as he had spoken those words, he discovered himself surrounded by the quiet night and complete solitude, hearing the wind's roar as it faded heavily through the forest. He stumbled against the rock and felt its cold, wet surface, while a drooping branch that had been completely ablaze sprinkled his cheek with the coldest dewdrops.

The next morning young Goodman Brown walked slowly into the street of Salem village, looking around him like a confused man. The good old minister was taking a walk along the graveyard to work up an appetite for breakfast and think about his sermon, and he gave a blessing, as he passed by, to Goodman Brown. He pulled away from the respected holy man as if trying to avoid a curse. Old Deacon Gookin was conducting family prayers, and the sacred words of his prayer could be heard through the open window. "What God does the wizard pray to?" said Goodman Brown. Goody Cloyse, that wonderful old Christian woman, stood in the early sunshine at her own window, teaching a little girl who had brought her a pint of morning's milk. Goodman Brown pulled the child away as if from the grip of the devil himself. Turning the corner by the meeting-house, he saw the head of Faith, with the pink ribbons, looking anxiously out, and breaking into such happiness at the sight of him that she skipped along the street and nearly kissed her husband in front of the whole village. But Goodman Brown looked sternly and sadly into her face, and walked on without a greeting.

Had Goodman Brown fallen asleep in the forest and only dreamed a wild dream of a witch-meeting?

Let it be so if you choose; but sadly, it was a dream that brought bad fortune to young Goodman Brown. He became a harsh, sorrowful, deeply troubled, and suspicious man—perhaps even a desperate one—from the night of that terrible dream. On Sunday, when the congregation sang a sacred psalm, he couldn't listen because a song of sin rang loudly in his ears and overwhelmed all the blessed music. When the minister preached from the pulpit with strength and passionate eloquence, with his hand on the open Bible, speaking of the holy truths of our faith, of saintly lives and victorious deaths, and of future joy or unspeakable suffering, Goodman Brown would turn pale, fearing that the roof might crash down upon the gray-haired blasphemer and his listeners. Often, awakening suddenly at midnight, he pulled away from Faith's embrace; and in the morning or evening, when the family knelt down to pray, he frowned and grumbled to himself, stared harshly at his wife, and looked away. And when he had lived a long life and was carried to his grave as a white-haired corpse, followed by Faith, now an elderly woman, and children and grandchildren, a large procession, along with many neighbors, they carved no hopeful words upon his tombstone, for his final hour was filled with darkness.

Rappaccini's Daughter

A young man named Giovanni Guasconti arrived long ago from southern Italy to study at the University of Padua. With only a few gold coins in his pocket, Giovanni rented a room in a tall, dark chamber within an old building that appeared grand enough to have once served as a Paduan nobleman's palace. Above the entrance, the structure still displayed the coat of arms of a family that had long since died out. The young stranger, who was well-versed in his country's greatest literary work, remembered that one of this family's ancestors—perhaps even a former resident of this very house—had been depicted by Dante as suffering eternal torment in his Inferno. These memories and connections, combined with the homesickness that naturally affects a young person living away from home for the first time, made Giovanni sigh deeply as he surveyed his bare and poorly furnished room.

"Holy Virgin, sir!" exclaimed old Dame Lisabetta, who, charmed by the young man's extraordinary physical beauty, was kindly trying to make the room more livable, "what a deep sigh to come from a young man's heart! Do you find this old house depressing? For heaven's sake, then, stick your head out the window, and you'll see sunshine just as bright as what you left behind in Naples."

Guasconti automatically followed the old woman's advice, though he couldn't entirely agree with her assessment that Padua's sunshine was as bright and cheerful as that of southern Italy. Whatever its quality, the sunlight streamed down onto a garden below his window and spread its nurturing warmth across an array of plants that appeared to have been tended with extraordinary attention.

"Does this garden belong to the house?" asked Giovanni.

"God forbid, sir, unless it produced better vegetables than any that grow there now," replied old Lisabetta. "No; that garden is tended by the very hands of Signor Giacomo Rappaccini, the renowned doctor, who, I assure you, has gained fame as far away as Naples. People say that he transforms these plants into medicines that are as powerful as magic. Often you might see the doctor himself at work, and perhaps the lady, his daughter, as well, collecting the unusual flowers that bloom in the garden."

The elderly woman had now completed everything she could do to improve the appearance of the room, and after entrusting the young man to the care of the saints, she left.

Giovanni still couldn't find anything better to do than gaze down into the garden below his window. Based on what he could see, he figured it must be one of those botanical gardens that had existed in Padua longer than anywhere else in Italy or the world. Or perhaps it had once been the private retreat of a wealthy family, since there were the remains of a marble fountain at the center, carved with exceptional skill, but so badly damaged that it was impossible to make out the original design from the jumbled pieces that remained. The water, though, kept bubbling and sparkling in the sunlight as cheerfully as always. A soft gurgling sound drifted up to the young man's window, making him feel as though the fountain were an eternal spirit singing its endless song, paying no attention to the changes happening around it, while one era had given it form in marble and another had scattered its fragile decorations across the ground. All around the pool where the water collected grew different plants that seemed to need plenty of moisture to feed their enormous leaves, and in some cases, magnificently gorgeous flowers. There was one bush in particular, planted in a marble container in the middle of the pool, that produced an abundance of purple blooms, each one gleaming with the brilliance and richness of a precious stone; and all of them together created such a dazzling display that it seemed capable of lighting up the entire garden, even without any sunshine. Every part of the soil was filled with plants and herbs that, while perhaps less beautiful, still showed signs of careful attention, as if each one possessed special properties known to the scientific mind that tended them. Some were planted in ornate urns decorated with ancient carvings, while others sat in ordinary garden pots; some crawled snake-like across the ground or climbed upward, using whatever support they could find. One plant had wound itself around a statue of Vertumnus, completely covering and concealing it in a curtain of drooping leaves, arranged so perfectly that it could have served as a model for a sculptor.

While Giovanni stood at the window, he heard rustling sounds coming from behind a curtain of leaves and realized that someone was working in the garden. The person's figure soon came into view, revealing not an ordinary laborer, but a tall, gaunt, pale, and unhealthy-looking man wearing the black robes of a scholar. He was past middle age, with gray hair, a thin gray beard, and a face distinctly marked by intelligence and refinement, though it appeared incapable of expressing much emotional warmth, even in his younger years.

Nothing could surpass the intense focus with which this scientific gardener examined every plant that grew along his path: it appeared as though he was peering into their deepest nature, making observations about their creative essence, and discovering why one leaf developed in this particular shape while another took on that form, and why certain flowers varied from one another in color and fragrance. However, despite this profound understanding on his part, there was no sense of closeness between himself and these plant life forms. Instead, he avoided actually touching them or directly breathing in their scents with a carefulness that struck Giovanni as quite unpleasant; the man's behavior was like someone walking among dangerous forces, such as wild animals, or poisonous serpents, or malevolent spirits, which, if he gave them even a moment's freedom, would bring some horrible disaster upon him. It was remarkably disturbing to the young man's mind to witness this atmosphere of uncertainty in someone tending a garden, that most basic and harmless of human activities, and which had been both the pleasure and work of humanity's innocent first parents. Was this garden, therefore, the Eden of today's world? And this man, with such an awareness of danger in what his own hands had cultivated to grow—was he the Adam?

The cautious gardener protected his hands with thick gloves while removing dead leaves and trimming back the overgrown branches of the bushes. These weren't his only protective measures. As he walked through the garden and approached the stunning plant that displayed its purple jewels next to the marble fountain, he covered his mouth and nose with a mask, as though all this beauty merely hid a more deadly threat. Finding his work still too risky, he stepped back, took off the mask, and shouted loudly, though his voice carried the weakness of someone suffering from an internal illness, "Beatrice! Beatrice!"

"Here I am, father. What do you need?" called out a rich and youthful voice from the window of the house across the way—a voice as rich as a tropical sunset, which made Giovanni, though he couldn't understand why, think of deep shades of purple or crimson and of heavily intoxicating perfumes. "Are you in the garden?"

"Yes, Beatrice," the gardener replied, "and I need your help."

Soon a young girl emerged from beneath a carved doorway, dressed with as much elegant taste as the most magnificent of the flowers, beautiful as the day itself, and with such deep and vibrant color that even one shade more would have been excessive. She appeared overflowing with life, health, and vitality; all of these qualities seemed bound and contained, as if tightly encircled in their abundance by her maiden's belt. Yet Giovanni's imagination must have become unhealthy as he gazed down into the garden; for the impression the lovely stranger made on him was as though she were another flower, the human counterpart of those plant ones, as beautiful as they were, more beautiful than the most magnificent among them, but still only to be touched while wearing gloves, and not to be approached without wearing a mask. As Beatrice walked down the garden pathway, it was noticeable that she touched and breathed in the fragrance of several plants that her father had most carefully avoided.

"Listen, Beatrice," he said, "look at how much essential care our most precious possession needs. But as broken down as I am, getting as close as the situation requires could cost me my life. From now on, I'm afraid this plant will have to be left entirely in your hands."

"I'll gladly take on this responsibility," the young woman called out again in her rich, melodious voice as she leaned toward the magnificent plant and spread her arms as though she wanted to embrace it. "Yes, my sister, my beautiful one, Beatrice will make it her duty to care for you and tend to your needs; and you will reward her with your kisses and fragrant breath, which means as much to her as the breath of life itself."

Then, with all the tenderness in her manner that was so strikingly expressed in her words, she busied herself with such care as the plant seemed to need; and Giovanni, at his high window, rubbed his eyes and almost wondered whether it was a girl tending her favorite flower, or one sister caring for another with loving devotion. The scene soon came to an end. Whether Dr. Rappaccini had completed his work in the garden, or his watchful eye had spotted the stranger's face, he now took his daughter's arm and withdrew. Night was already falling; heavy vapors seemed to rise from the plants and drift upward past the open window; and Giovanni, closing the shutters, went to his bed and dreamed of a magnificent flower and beautiful girl. Flower and maiden were different, and yet the same, and filled with some strange danger in either form.

But morning light has a way of correcting whatever mistakes our imagination or judgment might have led us to make during the evening hours, in the darkness of night, or under the unhealthy glow of moonlight. When Giovanni first woke up, his immediate impulse was to open the window and look down at the garden that had seemed so full of mysteries in his dreams. He felt surprised and somewhat embarrassed to discover how ordinary and realistic it actually appeared in the early sunlight that made the dewdrops on leaves and flowers sparkle, and while it enhanced the beauty of each unusual flower, it brought everything back within the realm of normal experience. The young man felt happy that in the middle of this lifeless city, he had the good fortune to overlook this area of beautiful and abundant plant life. It would serve, he told himself, as a symbolic language to maintain his connection with Nature. It's true that neither the pale and worry-worn Dr. Giacomo Rappaccini nor his radiant daughter could be seen at the moment, so Giovanni couldn't figure out how much of the strangeness he had attributed to both of them came from their actual characteristics and how much came from his imagination that created wonders out of nothing; but he was leaning toward taking a completely reasonable view of the entire situation.

During the day, he visited Signor Pietro Baglioni, a professor of medicine at the university and a physician of outstanding reputation, to whom Giovanni had brought a letter of introduction. The professor was an older man who seemed to have a warm personality and habits that could almost be described as cheerful. He invited the young man to stay for dinner and made himself very pleasant through his open and animated conversation, particularly after enjoying a bottle or two of Tuscan wine. Giovanni, thinking that men of science who lived in the same city would naturally be well-acquainted with each other, found a moment to bring up Dr. Rappaccini's name. However, the professor didn't respond with as much warmth as Giovanni had expected.

"It would be wrong for a teacher of the sacred art of medicine," said Professor Pietro Baglioni, responding to Giovanni's question, "to withhold proper and thoughtful praise of a physician as exceptionally skilled as Rappaccini; but, on the other hand, I would hardly satisfy my conscience if I allowed a worthy young man like yourself, Signor Giovanni, the son of an old friend, to develop mistaken ideas about a man who might someday hold your life and death in his hands. The truth is, our esteemed Dr. Rappaccini possesses as much knowledge as any member of the faculty—with perhaps one single exception—in Padua, or all of Italy; but there are certain serious concerns about his professional character."

"And what are they?" asked the young man.

"Does my friend Giovanni have some illness of the body or heart that makes him so curious about doctors?" the professor asked with a smile. "But regarding Rappaccini, people say about him—and I, who know the man well, can vouch for this being true—that he cares far more about science than he does about people. His patients interest him only as test subjects for some new experiment. He would sacrifice human life, including his own, or anything else most precious to him, just to add even the smallest bit to the vast collection of knowledge he has gathered."

"I think he's truly a terrible man," Guasconti said, mentally recalling Rappaccini's cold and purely intellectual demeanor. "And yet, respected professor, doesn't he possess a noble spirit? Are there many men capable of such a devoted love of science?"

"Absolutely not," the professor replied, with a hint of irritation in his voice; "at least, not unless they adopt more sensible approaches to medicine than those embraced by Rappaccini. His belief is that all healing properties can be found within those substances we call plant-based poisons. He grows these with his own hands, and people say he has even created new types of poison that are more terrifyingly deadly than anything Nature, without the help of this scholarly man, would have ever cursed the world with. That the good doctor causes less harm than one might expect when working with such dangerous materials is certainly true. From time to time, it must be admitted, he has accomplished, or appeared to accomplish, an extraordinary cure; but, to share my honest opinion with you, Signor Giovanni, he deserves little praise for such successful cases—they are probably just lucky accidents—but he should be held fully responsible for his failures, which can rightfully be considered entirely his doing."

The young man might have been more skeptical of Baglioni's views if he had known about the long-standing professional rivalry between him and Dr. Rappaccini, in which most people believed Rappaccini had come out ahead. If readers want to form their own opinion, they can look at the old printed documents from both sides that are kept in the medical department at the University of Padua.

"I don't know, most learned professor," Giovanni replied, after reflecting on what had been said about Rappaccini's single-minded devotion to science, "I don't know how deeply this physician may love his work; but certainly there is one thing more precious to him. He has a daughter."

"Aha!" the professor exclaimed with a laugh. "So now our friend Giovanni's secret is revealed. You've heard about this daughter, whom all the young men in Padua are crazy about, though fewer than six have ever been lucky enough to see her face. I know very little about Signora Beatrice except that Rappaccini is said to have taught her extensively in his science, and that, young and beautiful as her reputation claims, she's already qualified to hold a professor's position. Perhaps her father intends her for mine! There are other ridiculous rumors as well, not worth discussing or hearing. So now, Signor Giovanni, finish your glass of lachryma."

Giovanni returned to his room feeling somewhat affected by the wine he had drunk, which made his mind swirl with strange fantasies about Dr. Rappaccini and the beautiful Beatrice. Along the way, he happened to pass by a flower shop and bought a fresh bouquet of flowers.

Going up to his room, he sat down near the window, but stayed within the shadow cast by the thick wall, so he could look down into the garden without much chance of being seen. Everything below him was empty and quiet. The unusual plants were soaking up the sunlight, occasionally swaying gently toward each other, as if recognizing their shared nature and understanding. In the center, beside the broken fountain, stood the magnificent bush with its purple jewel-like flowers covering every branch; they sparkled in the air and reflected back from the depths of the pool, which seemed to overflow with brilliant color from the rich reflection soaking within it. Initially, as we mentioned, the garden was completely empty. Before long, however—just as Giovanni had both hoped and feared might happen—a figure appeared beneath the old carved doorway and walked down between the rows of plants, breathing in their different fragrances as if she were one of those creatures from ancient mythology that survived on sweet scents. Upon seeing Beatrice again, the young man was shocked to realize how much her beauty surpassed his memory of it; so radiant, so striking, was her presence, that she seemed to glow in the sunlight, and, as Giovanni whispered to himself, actually lit up the darker sections of the garden walkway. With her face now more visible than during their previous encounter, he was impressed by her expression of innocence and gentleness—traits that hadn't been part of his impression of her before, and which made him wonder again what kind of person she truly was. He also couldn't help but notice, or perhaps imagine, a similarity between the beautiful young woman and the splendid bush that draped its gem-like blossoms over the fountain—a likeness that Beatrice seemed to have playfully emphasized through both the style of her clothing and the colors she had chosen.

Approaching the shrub, she flung her arms wide with passionate intensity and pulled its branches into a close embrace—so close that her face disappeared into its leafy depths and her shining curls became tangled with the flowers.

"Give me your breath, my sister," Beatrice cried out, "because I feel weak from breathing ordinary air. And give me that flower of yours, which I'll carefully remove with the most gentle touch from its stem and hold close against my heart."

With these words, Rappaccini's beautiful daughter picked one of the most magnificent flowers from the shrub and was about to pin it to her dress. But then, unless the wine Giovanni had been drinking had clouded his judgment, something strange happened. A small orange lizard or chameleon happened to be crawling along the walkway right at Beatrice's feet. It seemed to Giovanni—though from where he was watching, he could barely have made out something so tiny—it seemed to him that a drop or two of liquid from the flower's broken stem fell onto the lizard's head. For a moment the creature writhed violently, then lay still in the sunlight. Beatrice noticed this extraordinary event and crossed herself with sadness but without shock; even so, she didn't hesitate to place the deadly flower against her chest. There it glowed brilliantly, shimmering with the stunning radiance of a jewel, giving her appearance and clothing the one perfect touch that nothing else on earth could have provided. But Giovanni, hidden in the shadows of his window, leaned forward and pulled back, whispering and shaking.

"Am I awake? Do I still have my senses?" he asked himself. "What kind of being is this? Should I call her beautiful, or unspeakably terrifying?"

Beatrice now wandered casually through the garden, moving closer beneath Giovanni's window, forcing him to lean his head completely out from his hiding place to satisfy the intense and agonizing curiosity she stirred in him. At that moment, a beautiful insect flew over the garden wall; it had perhaps drifted through the city and discovered no flowers or greenery among those ancient dwelling places of humanity until the heavy fragrances of Dr. Rappaccini's plants had drawn it from a distance. Without landing on the flowers, this winged creature of light appeared to be drawn to Beatrice, hovering in the air and fluttering around her head. At this point, it seemed impossible that Giovanni Guasconti's eyes were not playing tricks on him. Whatever the case might be, he imagined that while Beatrice gazed at the insect with innocent joy, it grew weak and dropped at her feet; its brilliant wings trembled; it was dead—for no reason he could determine, except perhaps the air from her breathing. Once again Beatrice made the sign of the cross and let out a deep sigh as she leaned over the lifeless insect.

A sudden movement from Giovanni caught her attention and made her look toward the window. There she saw the handsome face of the young man—more Greek than Italian in appearance, with light, well-proportioned features and golden highlights gleaming in his curly hair—looking down at her as if he were floating in the air above. Barely aware of his actions, Giovanni dropped the bouquet he had been holding in his hand.

"Madam," he said, "these are pure and healthy flowers. Wear them for Giovanni Guasconti's sake."

"Thank you, sir," Beatrice replied, her rich voice flowing like a stream of music, accompanied by a joyful expression that was part childlike and part womanly. "I accept your gift and would gladly repay it with this precious purple flower, but if I throw it into the air, it won't reach you. So Mr. Guasconti will have to be satisfied with my gratitude."

She picked up the bouquet from the ground, and then, as if secretly embarrassed for abandoning her modest restraint to acknowledge a stranger's greeting, hurried quickly home through the garden. Though only moments had passed, it appeared to Giovanni, as she was about to disappear beneath the carved doorway, that his lovely bouquet was already starting to wilt in her hands. It was a foolish notion; there was no way to tell a withered flower from a fresh one from such a great distance.

For many days following this event, the young man stayed away from the window that overlooked Dr. Rappaccini's garden, as though something hideous and terrifying might have destroyed his vision if he had accidentally looked out. He was aware that he had somehow placed himself under the influence of a mysterious force through the connection he had established with Beatrice. The smartest thing to do, if his heart was truly at risk, would have been to leave his rooms and Padua immediately; the second best option would have been to get used to seeing Beatrice in normal daylight as much as possible—thereby forcing her firmly and methodically into the realm of ordinary experience. Most foolish of all, while staying away from seeing her, Giovanni should not have remained so close to this remarkable woman that their nearness and the mere possibility of interaction would give some form and reality to the wild fantasies that his imagination constantly created. Guasconti did not have a profound heart—or at least, its depths had not been explored at this time; but he possessed a lively imagination and a passionate southern nature that grew more intense with each passing moment. Whether or not Beatrice actually had those frightening qualities, that deadly breath, the connection with those beautiful yet poisonous flowers that Giovanni's observations had suggested, she had certainly introduced a powerful and dangerous toxin into his being. It was not love, though her stunning beauty drove him to madness; nor was it horror, even as he imagined her soul to be filled with the same harmful essence that appeared to flow through her body; instead, it was a chaotic mixture of both love and horror that contained elements of each, burning like one emotion while trembling like the other. Giovanni didn't know what he should fear; he understood even less what he should hope for; yet hope and fear waged constant battle in his chest, each defeating the other in turn before rising again to continue the fight. Fortunate are all pure emotions, whether they are dark or bright! It is the disturbing combination of both that creates the blazing light of hell itself.

Sometimes he tried to calm his restless mind by walking quickly through the streets of Padua or outside the city walls: his steps matched the pounding in his head, so the walk often turned into a run. One day he was stopped; a heavy-set man grabbed his arm, having turned around after recognizing the young man and used considerable effort to catch up with him.

"Mr. Giovanni! Wait, my young friend!" he called out. "Have you forgotten me? That would certainly be understandable if I had changed as much as you have."

It was Baglioni, the same person Giovanni had been avoiding ever since their initial encounter, worried that the professor's sharp insight would probe too deeply into his private matters. Trying to pull himself together, he gazed out frantically from his internal thoughts to the external world and spoke as if he were caught in a dream.

"Yes; I am Giovanni Guasconti. You are Professor Pietro Baglioni. Now let me pass!"

"Not yet, not yet, Mr. Giovanni Guasconti," said the professor, smiling, but at the same time studying the young man with a serious look. "What! Did I grow up alongside your father? And should his son walk past me like a stranger on these old streets of Padua? Wait a moment, Mr. Giovanni; we need to have a conversation before we go our separate ways."

"Quickly, then, most respected professor, quickly," said Giovanni, with feverish impatience. "Can't you see that I'm in a hurry?"

Now, while he was speaking, a man dressed in black came walking down the street, hunched over and moving weakly like someone in poor health. His face was completely covered with an extremely sickly and pale yellow color, but it was so filled with an expression of sharp and alert intelligence that someone watching might easily have ignored his purely physical appearance and noticed only this remarkable mental energy. As he walked by, this person gave Baglioni a cold and distant greeting, but stared at Giovanni with such intensity that it seemed to draw out whatever was noteworthy about him. Still, there was a strange detachment in his gaze, as if he was taking only a scientific interest in the young man rather than a personal one.

"It's Dr. Rappaccini!" the professor whispered after the stranger had walked by. "Has he ever seen your face before?"

"Not that I know," Giovanni replied, startled by the name.

"He HAS seen you! He must have seen you!" Baglioni said urgently. "For some reason, this scientist is studying you. I recognize that expression of his! It's the same cold look that lights up his face when he leans over a bird, a mouse, or a butterfly that he has killed with a flower's fragrance as part of some experiment. It's a look as profound as Nature itself, but lacking Nature's warmth and love. Mr. Giovanni, I would bet my life on it—you are the subject of one of Rappaccini's experiments!"

"Are you trying to make me look like an idiot?" Giovanni shouted angrily. "THAT, professor, would be a dangerous experiment."

"Be patient! Be patient!" replied the unshakeable professor. "I'm telling you, my poor Giovanni, that Rappaccini has a scientific interest in you. You've fallen into dangerous hands! And what about Signora Beatrice—what role does she play in this mystery?"

But Guasconti found Baglioni's persistence unbearable, so he broke away at this point and left before the professor could grab his arm again. The professor watched the young man intently as he departed and shook his head.

"This cannot be allowed," Baglioni said to himself. "The young man is the son of my old friend, and he must not suffer any harm that medical knowledge can prevent. Furthermore, it's an intolerable act of arrogance for Rappaccini to steal the boy from under my nose, so to speak, and use him for his diabolical experiments. This daughter of his! Something must be done about her. Perhaps, most scholarly Rappaccini, I can defeat you in ways you never imagine!"

Meanwhile Giovanni had taken a roundabout path, and eventually found himself at the door of his apartment. As he stepped across the threshold he was greeted by old Lisabetta, who grinned and beamed, and was clearly eager to catch his attention; unsuccessfully, however, as the surge of his emotions had temporarily settled into a cold and empty numbness. He directed his gaze directly upon the wrinkled face that was creasing itself into a smile, but appeared not to see it. The old woman, therefore, grabbed hold of his cloak.

"Sir! Sir!" she whispered, still wearing a smile that stretched across her entire face, making it look like a grotesque wooden carving that had been darkened by centuries of age. "Listen, sir! There's a private entrance into the garden!"

"What did you say?" Giovanni exclaimed, spinning around quickly, like something lifeless suddenly bursting into frantic activity. "A private entrance into Dr. Rappaccini's garden?"

"Quiet! Quiet! Don't speak so loudly!" Lisabetta whispered, placing her hand over his mouth. "Yes, into the respected doctor's garden, where you can see all his beautiful plants and shrubs. Many young men in Padua would pay handsomely to be allowed among those flowers."

Giovanni placed a gold coin in her hand.

"Show me the way," he said.

A thought crossed his mind, likely sparked by his conversation with Baglioni, that old Lisabetta's interference might somehow be connected to the scheme—whatever its true nature—that the professor seemed to believe Dr.

Rappaccini was drawing him into. But even though this suspicion troubled Giovanni, it wasn't enough to hold him back. The moment he realized he might be able to approach Beatrice, it felt like an absolute requirement for his very existence. It didn't matter whether she was an angel or a demon; he was hopelessly caught in her influence and had to follow the force that pulled him forward in tightening circles toward an outcome he couldn't predict. Yet strangely, a sudden uncertainty came over him about whether this overwhelming fascination of his might be an illusion— whether it was truly deep and genuine enough to justify putting himself in such an unpredictable situation, or whether it was simply the imagination of a young man's mind, barely connected to his heart at all.

He stopped, wavered, turned halfway around, but then continued forward again. His aged guide led him through several dim corridors, and eventually unlocked a door, which, when opened, revealed the sight and sound of rustling leaves, with fragmented sunlight flickering through them. Giovanni stepped outside, and, pushing himself through the tangle of a bush that wound its branches over the concealed entrance, found himself standing beneath his own window in the open space of Dr. Rappaccini's garden.

How often does it happen that when impossible things actually occur and dreams transform from vague hopes into real experiences, we discover ourselves feeling calm and even emotionally detached in situations that would have driven us wild with excitement or despair if we had imagined them beforehand! Fate enjoys frustrating us in this way. Strong emotions will pick their own moment to overwhelm us, and they drag their feet when the perfect arrangement of circumstances seems to call for their arrival. This was exactly what happened with Giovanni. Day after day his heart had raced with fevered anticipation at the unlikely possibility of meeting Beatrice face to face, of standing with her right there in this very garden, warming himself in the radiant glow of her beauty, and discovering through her direct gaze the secret that he believed held the key to understanding his own life. But now there was an odd and poorly timed sense of calm filling his chest. He looked around the garden to see if Beatrice or her father were anywhere nearby, and when he realized he was alone, he started examining the plants with careful attention.

The appearance of each and every one of them troubled him; their splendor appeared fierce, intense, and even unnatural. There was scarcely a single bush that a traveler, wandering alone through a forest, wouldn't have been shocked to discover growing wild, as though a supernatural face had stared at him from the undergrowth. Many would have also disturbed a sensitive nature through their artificial appearance, suggesting there had been such mixing and, in a sense, corruption of different plant species that what resulted was no longer God's creation, but rather the grotesque product of humanity's corrupted imagination, radiating only a sinister imitation of beauty. They were likely the outcome of experimentation, which in a few instances had managed to blend individually beautiful plants into a hybrid possessing the dubious and threatening quality that characterized the entire garden's growth. In short, Giovanni identified only two or three plants in the collection, and these were varieties he knew well to be toxic. While occupied with these thoughts he heard the whisper of silk fabric, and turning around, saw Beatrice appearing from beneath the carved doorway.

Giovanni hadn't thought about how he should behave; whether he should apologize for trespassing in the garden, or act as if he was there with the knowledge, if not the invitation, of Dr. Rappaccini or his daughter; but Beatrice's manner put him at ease, though it still left him wondering how he had gotten in. She walked gracefully along the path and met him near the broken fountain. There was surprise on her face, but it was brightened by a simple and kind expression of pleasure.

"You're an expert when it comes to flowers, sir," Beatrice said with a smile, referring to the bouquet he had thrown to her from the window. "So it's no surprise that seeing my father's rare collection would make you want to get a closer look. If he were here, he could share many fascinating and unusual details about the nature and behavior of these plants, since he's devoted his entire life to studying them, and this garden is his whole world."

"And you, lady," Giovanni remarked, "if the rumors are true, you also possess deep knowledge of the powers represented by these beautiful flowers and fragrant scents. If you would honor me by becoming my teacher, I would be a more eager student than if I were instructed by Signor Rappaccini himself."

"Are there such idle rumors?" asked Beatrice, with the music of a pleasant laugh. "Do people say that I am skilled in my father's science of plants? What a joke that is! No; though I have grown up among these flowers, I know no more of them than their colors and fragrance; and sometimes I think I would gladly rid myself of even that small knowledge. There are many flowers here, and those not the least brilliant, that shock and offend me when they meet my eye. But please, sir, do not believe these stories about my science. Believe nothing of me except what you see with your own eyes."

"Do I really have to believe everything I've witnessed myself?" Giovanni asked directly, as memories of past events made him recoil. "No, signora; you're asking too little of me. Tell me to believe nothing except what you say with your own words."

It seemed that Beatrice understood him. A deep blush spread across her cheek, but she looked directly into Giovanni's eyes and met his gaze of troubled suspicion with regal pride.

"I'm asking you to do this, sir," she responded. "Forget whatever you might have imagined about me. Even if it seems real to your eyes and other senses, it could still be fundamentally untrue; but the words that come from Beatrice Rappaccini's lips are genuine from the very core of my heart to the surface. You can trust those words."

A passionate intensity radiated from her entire being and shone into Giovanni's awareness like the light of truth itself; but as she spoke, there was a sweet scent in the air surrounding her, luxurious and enchanting, though fleeting, which the young man, due to some unexplainable hesitation, barely dared to breathe in. It could have been the smell of the flowers. Might it have been Beatrice's breath that perfumed her words with such unusual richness, as though she had soaked them in her very heart? A moment of weakness swept over Giovanni like a passing shadow and then disappeared; he felt as though he was looking through the beautiful girl's eyes directly into her clear soul, and experienced no further doubt or fear.

The hint of passion that had colored Beatrice's behavior disappeared; she became cheerful, and seemed to find genuine pleasure in her conversation with the young man, much like what a girl from an isolated island might have experienced while talking with a traveler from the civilized world. Clearly her knowledge of life had been limited to the boundaries of that garden. She spoke about things as basic as daylight or summer clouds, and then asked questions about the city, or Giovanni's faraway home, his friends, his mother, and his sisters—questions that showed such isolation, and such unfamiliarity with customs and social conventions, that Giovanni answered as if speaking to a child. Her spirit flowed out before him like a fresh stream that was just seeing sunlight for the first time and marveling at the reflections of earth and sky that were cast into its depths. There came thoughts, too, from a profound source, and imaginings of jewel-like brilliance, as if diamonds and rubies sparkled upward among the bubbles of the fountain. Now and then there flashed across the young man's mind a feeling of amazement that he should be walking beside the person who had so affected his imagination, whom he had pictured in such shades of terror, in whom he had actually seen such displays of frightening qualities,—that he should be talking with Beatrice like a brother, and should find her so human and so girlish. But such thoughts were only brief; the impact of her character was too genuine not to become familiar immediately.

During their casual stroll through the garden, they had wandered along its paths and, after taking many turns through the walkways, arrived at the broken fountain where the magnificent plant grew with its collection of brilliant flowers. The shrub released a fragrance that Giovanni immediately recognized as the same scent he had noticed on Beatrice's breath, though this was far more intense. When she looked at the plant, Giovanni saw her place her hand against her chest as though her heart had begun beating rapidly and with discomfort.

"For the first time in my life," she whispered to the shrub, "I had forgotten you."

"I remember, signora," Giovanni said, "that you once promised to give me one of these living gems as a reward for the bouquet I was bold enough to throw at your feet. Please allow me now to pick one as a keepsake of our meeting."

He took a step toward the shrub with his hand outstretched; but Beatrice rushed forward, letting out a scream that pierced his heart like a blade. She grabbed his hand and pulled it back with all the strength of her delicate frame. Giovanni felt her touch sending shivers through his entire body.

"Don't touch it!" she cried out in anguish. "Not if your life depends on it! It's deadly!"

Then, covering her face, she ran away from him and disappeared beneath the carved doorway. As Giovanni watched her go, he saw the gaunt figure and pale, intelligent face of Dr. Rappaccini, who had been observing the scene from the shadows of the entrance for who knows how long.

As soon as Guasconti found himself alone in his room, Beatrice's image returned to fill his passionate thoughts, wrapped in all the enchantment that had been building around it since he first saw her, and now also filled with the tender warmth of youthful femininity. She was human; her character possessed all the gentle and feminine traits; she deserved to be adored; she was surely capable, on her side, of love's greatest heights and heroism. Those signs that he had previously viewed as evidence of some terrible abnormality in her physical and moral nature were now either forgotten, or through passion's clever reasoning transformed into a golden crown of magic, making Beatrice all the more wonderful because she was so extraordinary.

Whatever had seemed ugly now appeared beautiful; or, if it couldn't undergo such a transformation, it slipped away and concealed itself among those vague half-formed thoughts that crowd the shadowy realm beyond our clear awareness. This is how he passed the night, not falling asleep until dawn had started to rouse the sleeping flowers in Dr. Rappaccini's garden, where Giovanni's dreams undoubtedly carried him. The sun rose at its appointed time, and casting its rays upon the young man's eyelids, woke him to a feeling of pain. When fully awakened, he became aware of a burning and stinging torment in his hand—in his right hand—the very hand that Beatrice had clasped in hers when he was about to pick one of the jewel-like flowers. On the back of that hand there was now a purple mark resembling four small fingers, and the outline of a slender thumb upon his wrist.

Oh, how stubbornly love clings on—or even that clever illusion of love that thrives in our imagination but never truly takes root in the heart—how persistently it maintains its hold until the moment arrives when it must dissolve into nothing! Giovanni wrapped a handkerchief around his hand and wondered what harmful creature had stung him, and quickly forgot his pain as he lost himself in thoughts of Beatrice.

After the first meeting, a second encounter followed as part of what we call destiny. Then came a third, a fourth, and eventually meeting Beatrice in the garden was no longer just an event in Giovanni's daily routine, but became the entire world in which he lived; the anticipation and memories of that blissful time filled all his remaining hours. The same was true for Rappaccini's daughter. She waited eagerly for the young man to appear and rushed to his side with complete trust, as if they had been childhood friends from their earliest years—as if they were still those same playmates. If, by some unusual circumstance, he didn't arrive at their usual time, she would stand beneath his window and let the rich sweetness of her voice drift up to surround him in his room and resonate throughout his heart: "Giovanni! Giovanni! Why do you delay? Come down!" And down he would hurry into that paradise of deadly flowers.

But despite all this close familiarity, Beatrice still maintained a certain distance in her behavior, so strictly and consistently that the thought of crossing that boundary barely entered his mind. By every visible sign, they were in love; they had exchanged loving looks with eyes that carried the sacred secret from the depths of one soul to the depths of another, as if it were too holy to be spoken aloud; they had even declared their love in those bursts of passion when their spirits poured forth in spoken words like flames of long-concealed fire; and yet there had been no kiss, no holding of hands, nor any gentle touch that love demands and makes sacred. He had never touched even one of the shining curls of her hair; her clothing—so clear was the physical distance between them—had never brushed against him in the wind. On the rare occasions when Giovanni seemed about to cross that line, Beatrice became so sad, so serious, and showed such a look of lonely separation, trembling at itself, that no spoken words were needed to push him away. During these moments he was shocked by the terrible doubts that emerged, like monsters, from the depths of his heart and confronted him directly; his love became weak and pale like morning fog, while only his uncertainties felt real. But when Beatrice's face lit up again after the brief darkness, she was instantly changed from the mysterious, doubtful person he had observed with such fear and dread; she was now the beautiful and innocent girl whom he felt his soul recognized with a certainty greater than any other understanding.

A significant amount of time had passed since Giovanni's last encounter with Baglioni. One morning, though, he was unpleasantly startled by a visit from the professor, whom he had barely considered for entire weeks and would have gladly forgotten for even longer. Consumed as he had been for so long by an overwhelming passion, he could endure no company except on the condition that they completely understood his current emotional state. Such understanding was not something he could expect from Professor Baglioni.

The visitor made casual conversation for a few minutes about the latest gossip from the city and the university, then shifted to a different subject.

"I've been reading an old classic author recently," he said, "and I came across a story that fascinated me deeply. You might recall it. It tells of an Indian prince who sent a beautiful woman as a gift to Alexander the Great. She was as lovely as the dawn and as magnificent as the sunset; but what particularly set her apart was a certain rich fragrance in her breath—more luxurious than a garden of Persian roses. Alexander, as would be expected of a young conqueror, fell in love immediately with this stunning stranger; but a wise physician who happened to be there uncovered a terrible secret about her."

"And what was that?" asked Giovanni, looking down to avoid meeting the professor's gaze.

"This beautiful woman," Baglioni went on with emphasis, "had been fed poisons from the moment she was born, until her entire being was so saturated with them that she herself had become the most lethal poison that ever existed. Poison was the very essence of her life. With the rich fragrance of her breath, she contaminated the air itself. Her love would have been poison—her embrace would have meant death. Isn't this an extraordinary story?"

"A childish fable," Giovanni replied, nervously jumping up from his chair. "I'm amazed that you find time to read such nonsense among your more serious studies."

"By the way," said the professor, looking nervously around him, "what unusual fragrance is this in your room? Is it the perfume from your gloves? It's faint, but delightful; and yet, after all, not really pleasant. If I were to breathe it for long, I think it would make me sick. It's like the breath of a flower; but I don't see any flowers in the room."

"There aren't any," Giovanni replied, his face turning pale as the professor spoke. "And I don't think there's any fragrance except in your imagination. Scents, being a kind of element that combines the physical and the spiritual, tend to deceive us this way. The memory of a perfume, just the thought of it, can easily be mistaken for something that's actually there."

"Yes, but my clear thinking doesn't usually play such tricks on me," said Baglioni. "And if I were to imagine any kind of smell, it would be that of some foul pharmacy drug that my fingers are probably stained with. Our respected friend Rappaccini, as I've heard, infuses his medicines with fragrances richer than those of Arabia. No doubt the beautiful and scholarly Signora Beatrice would also treat her patients with potions as sweet as a young woman's breath— but cursed is the man who tastes them!"

Giovanni's face showed many conflicting emotions. The way the professor spoke about Rappaccini's pure and beautiful daughter was torment to his soul; yet the suggestion of a view of her character that contradicted his own gave immediate clarity to a thousand vague suspicions, which now leered at him like countless demons. But he fought hard to suppress them and to respond to Baglioni with a true lover's complete faith.

"Professor," he said, "you were my father's friend, and perhaps you also intend to be a friend to his son. I want to feel nothing but respect and reverence for you, but please understand, sir, that there's one topic we must not discuss. You don't know Signora Beatrice. Therefore, you cannot understand the harm—the sacrilege, I might even call it—that any careless or hurtful word inflicts upon her character."

"Giovanni! My poor Giovanni!" the professor replied, his face showing calm compassion. "I know this unfortunate girl far better than you do. You're going to hear the truth about the poisoner Rappaccini and his toxic daughter—yes, as poisonous as she is beautiful. Listen to me, because even if you harm an old man like me, you won't stop me from speaking. That ancient legend about the Indian woman has been made real through Rappaccini's profound and deadly science, embodied in the lovely Beatrice."

Giovanni groaned and covered his face with his hands.

"Her father," Baglioni went on, "wasn't held back by natural parental love from sacrificing his child in this terrible way as a victim of his mad passion for science; because, to be fair to him, he is as dedicated a scientist as any who ever distilled his own heart in a laboratory vessel. So what will happen to you? Without question, you have been chosen as the subject of some new experiment. Maybe the outcome will be death; maybe something even more dreadful. Rappaccini, with what he calls the advancement of science driving him, will stop at nothing."

"It's a dream," Giovanni whispered to himself; "it has to be a dream."

"But," the professor continued, "stay hopeful, my friend's son. There's still time to save her. We might even manage to bring this unfortunate girl back to normal human nature, away from the unnatural state her father's obsession has trapped her in. Look at this small silver container! It was crafted by the famous Benvenuto Cellini himself, and it's beautiful enough to be a romantic gift for the most stunning woman in all of Italy. However, what's inside is priceless. Just one small taste of this remedy would have made even the deadliest poisons used by the Borgias completely harmless. Don't doubt that it will work just as well against Rappaccini's toxins. Give this container and the valuable liquid it holds to your Beatrice, and wait with hope for what happens next."

Baglioni placed a small, beautifully crafted silver vial on the table and left, allowing his words to sink in and influence the young man's thoughts.

"We'll still outsmart Rappaccini," he thought, chuckling to himself as he walked down the stairs. "But let's be honest about him—he's an extraordinary man, truly extraordinary. However, he's a dangerous quack in his methods, and for that reason, those of us who honor the time-tested principles of the medical profession cannot tolerate him."

Throughout Giovanni's entire relationship with Beatrice, he had sometimes, as we have mentioned, been troubled by dark suspicions about her character; yet she had so completely presented herself to him as a simple, natural, deeply loving, and innocent person, that the picture now presented by Professor Baglioni seemed as strange and unbelievable as if it contradicted his own initial understanding. Certainly, there were disturbing memories connected with his first glimpses of the beautiful girl; he could not entirely forget the bouquet that wilted in her hands, and the insect that died in the bright air, with no apparent cause except the scent of her breath. These incidents, however, fading in the pure light of her character, no longer had the power of facts, but were recognized as mistaken illusions, regardless of whatever evidence from his senses they might seem to provide. There is something more true and more real than what we can see with our eyes and touch with our fingers. On such better evidence Giovanni had built his trust in Beatrice, though more through the inevitable power of her noble qualities than through any deep and generous faith on his part. But now his spirit was unable to maintain itself at the height to which the early excitement of passion had lifted it; he fell down, crawling among earthly doubts, and stained with them the pure whiteness of Beatrice's image. Not that he abandoned her; he simply distrusted. He decided to create some decisive test that would satisfy him, once and for all, whether there were those terrible peculiarities in her physical nature which could not be assumed to exist without some corresponding monstrosity of soul. His eyes, looking down from far away, might have deceived him regarding the lizard, the insect, and the flowers; but if he could witness, at the distance of a few steps, the sudden destruction of one fresh and healthy flower in Beatrice's hand, there would be no room for further question. With this idea he hurried to the florist's and bought a bouquet that was still decorated with the morning dewdrops.

It was now the usual time for his daily meeting with Beatrice. Before going down into the garden, Giovanni made sure to look at himself in the mirror—a vanity that could be expected from a handsome young man, yet, showing itself at such a troubled and anxious moment, it revealed a certain lack of depth in his feelings and dishonesty in his character. He did look at himself, however, and told himself that his features had never before held such rich beauty, nor had his eyes ever shown such liveliness, nor his cheeks ever displayed such a warm glow of abundant life.

"At least," he thought, "her poison hasn't worked its way into my system yet. I'm not some flower that will wither and die in her hands."

With that thought, he turned his gaze to the bouquet, which he had never once set down from his hand. A wave of unexplainable terror coursed through his body when he noticed that those moisture-laden flowers were already starting to wilt; they had the appearance of things that had been vibrant and beautiful yesterday. Giovanni became as pale as marble, and remained frozen before the mirror, gazing at his own reflection as if looking at the image of something terrifying. He recalled Baglioni's comment about the scent that seemed to fill the room. It must have been the poison in his breath! Then he trembled—trembled at himself. Emerging from his daze, he started to observe with fascinated attention a spider that was actively working to construct its web from the old decorative molding of the room, weaving back and forth through the intricate pattern of interconnected strands—as energetic and lively a spider as ever hung from an aged ceiling. Giovanni leaned toward the creature, and released a deep, prolonged breath. The spider abruptly stopped its labor; the web shook with a quiver that began in the body of the tiny craftsman. Once more Giovanni exhaled a breath, deeper, longer, and filled with a poisonous emotion from his heart: he did not know whether he was evil, or simply desperate. The spider made a violent clutching motion with its legs and hung lifeless across the window.

"Cursed! Cursed!" Giovanni muttered to himself. "Have you become so poisonous that this deadly insect dies from your breath?"

At that moment, a rich, sweet voice drifted up from the garden.

"Giovanni! Giovanni! It's past the hour! Why are you delaying? Come down!"

"Yes," Giovanni muttered once more. "She's the only person my breath can't kill! If only it could!"

He rushed down, and in an instant was standing before the bright and loving eyes of Beatrice. A moment ago his anger and despair had been so intense that he could have wanted nothing more than to destroy her with a single look; but with her actual presence there came influences which had too real an existence to be immediately cast aside: memories of the delicate and gentle power of her feminine nature, which had so often surrounded him in a spiritual calm; memories of many a sacred and passionate outpouring of her heart, when the pure fountain had been opened from its depths and made visible in its clarity to his mind's eye; memories which, had Giovanni known how to value them, would have convinced him that all this terrible mystery was but an earthly illusion, and that, whatever cloud of evil might seem to have gathered over her, the real Beatrice was a heavenly angel. Incapable as he was of such profound faith, still her presence had not completely lost its power. Giovanni's fury was reduced to an expression of brooding numbness. Beatrice, with a quick spiritual sense, immediately felt that there was a chasm of darkness between them which neither he nor she could cross. They walked on together, sad and silent, and came thus to the marble fountain and to its pool of water on the ground, in the midst of which grew the shrub that bore jewel-like blossoms.

Giovanni was frightened at the eager pleasure—the hunger, as it were—with which he found himself breathing in the fragrance of the flowers.

"Beatrice," he asked suddenly, "where did this shrub come from?"

"My father created it," she replied simply.

"Created it! Created it!" Giovanni said again. "What do you mean, Beatrice?"

"He is a man who knows Nature's secrets in a terrifying way," Beatrice answered; "and when I took my first breath, this plant emerged from the earth, born from his scientific knowledge and his mind, while I was merely his human daughter. Don't go near it!" she continued, watching in fear as Giovanni moved closer to the plant. "It possesses qualities you can't even imagine. But I, my dearest Giovanni—I grew up and flourished alongside the plant and was fed by its breath. It became my sister, and I loved it with human feelings; because, sadly—haven't you guessed it?— there was a terrible fate."

Here Giovanni frowned at her so intensely that Beatrice stopped speaking and began to tremble. However, her trust in his gentle nature comforted her and caused her to feel embarrassed that she had questioned him, even for a moment.

"There was a terrible curse," she went on, "caused by my father's deadly obsession with science, which cut me off from all human companionship. Until Heaven sent you, dearest Giovanni, oh, how lonely your poor Beatrice was!"

"Was it a harsh fate?" asked Giovanni, looking directly at her.

"Only recently have I understood how difficult it was," she replied gently. "Oh, yes; but my heart was numb, and therefore calm."

Giovanni's anger erupted from his brooding darkness like lightning bursting from a storm cloud.

"You cursed creature!" he shouted, his voice filled with poisonous contempt and rage. "And because you found your isolation unbearable, you have cut me off from all of life's warmth as well and lured me into your realm of indescribable terror!"

"Giovanni!" Beatrice cried out, fixing her large, luminous eyes on his face. The power behind his words hadn't penetrated her thoughts; she was simply stunned.

"Yes, you poisonous creature!" Giovanni repeated, consumed with rage. "You have done this! You have destroyed me! You have filled my veins with poison! You have made me as hateful, as ugly, as repulsive and deadly a creature as yourself—a world's wonder of hideous monstrosity! Now, if our breath is fortunately as fatal to ourselves as it is to all others, let us press our lips together in one kiss of unspeakable hatred, and die!"

"What has happened to me?" whispered Beatrice, with a quiet groan from deep within her heart. "Holy Virgin, have mercy on me, a poor heartbroken child!"

"You—do you pray?" Giovanni cried out, his voice still filled with the same demonic contempt. "Your very prayers, as they leave your lips, poison the air with death. Yes, yes; let us pray! Let us go to church and dip our fingers in the holy water at the entrance! Those who come after us will die as if struck by plague! Let us make the sign of the cross in the air! It will be like spreading curses throughout the world in the form of sacred symbols!"

"Giovanni," said Beatrice calmly, for her grief had moved beyond passion, "why do you join with me in speaking such terrible words? I am indeed the horrible thing you call me. But you—what do you have to do with this, except to shudder once more at my hideous misery, then leave the garden and rejoin your fellow humans, and forget that such a monster as poor Beatrice ever crawled upon this earth?"

"Are you pretending not to know?" asked Giovanni, scowling at her. "Look! This is the power I have gained from the pure daughter of Rappaccini."

A cloud of summer insects darted through the air, drawn by the fragrant scents of flowers in the deadly garden. They swarmed around Giovanni's head, clearly pulled toward him by the same force that had momentarily brought them near several of the plants. He exhaled among them and looked at Beatrice with a bitter smile as at least twenty insects dropped dead to the ground.

"I can see it! I can see it!" Beatrice cried out. "It's my father's deadly science! No, no, Giovanni; it wasn't me! Never! Never! I only dreamed of loving you and being with you for a short while, and then letting you go, keeping only your memory in my heart. Because, Giovanni, believe me, even though my body feeds on poison, my soul belongs to God and hungers for love as its daily nourishment. But my father—he has bound us together in this terrible connection. Yes, reject me, step on me, kill me! Oh, what is death compared to words like yours? But it wasn't me. Not for all the happiness in the world would I have done such a thing."

Giovanni's passion had spent itself in the words that poured from his lips. A feeling now washed over him—sorrowful yet touched with tenderness—of the intimate and unique bond between Beatrice and himself. They existed, it seemed, in complete isolation, a loneliness that would remain unchanged even amid the thickest crowd of humanity. Should not this desert of people surrounding them draw this isolated pair closer together? If they were harsh with each other, who else would show them kindness? Moreover, Giovanni thought, might there not still be hope that he could return to the boundaries of normal existence and guide Beatrice—the saved Beatrice—by the hand? Oh, what a weak, selfish, and worthless soul to imagine that earthly union and earthly joy could be possible after such profound love had been so cruelly wounded as Beatrice's love was by Giovanni's devastating words! No, no; such hope could not exist. She would have to pass painfully, with that shattered heart, beyond the boundaries of Time—she would have to heal her wounds in some fountain of paradise, and lose her sorrow in the radiance of eternity, and THERE find peace.

But Giovanni didn't know it.

"Dear Beatrice," he said, moving closer to her, while she pulled back as she always did when he approached, though now for a different reason, "dearest Beatrice, our situation isn't hopeless yet. Look! There's a medicine here, powerful, as a knowledgeable doctor has promised me, and almost miraculous in how well it works. It's made from ingredients that are completely opposite to those your terrible father used to bring this disaster upon you and me. It's made from blessed herbs. Shouldn't we drink it together, and in doing so cleanse ourselves of this evil?"

"Give it to me!" said Beatrice, reaching out her hand to take the small silver bottle that Giovanni pulled from his chest. She added, with particular emphasis, "I will drink it; but you must wait to see what happens."

She brought Baglioni's antidote to her lips, and at that exact moment, Rappaccini's figure appeared from the doorway and walked slowly toward the marble fountain. As he approached, the pale scientist appeared to look at the beautiful young man and woman with a triumphant expression, like an artist who had devoted his entire life to creating a painting or sculpture and was finally pleased with what he had accomplished. He stopped walking; his hunched figure straightened with a sense of conscious power; he extended his hands over them in the gesture of a father asking for a blessing upon his children; but these were the very same hands that had poured poison into the course of their lives. Giovanni shook with fear. Beatrice trembled anxiously and placed her hand over her heart.

"My daughter," said Rappaccini, "you are no longer alone in the world. Pick one of those precious gems from your sister shrub and ask your bridegroom to wear it on his chest. It will not hurt him now. My science and the connection between you and him have worked so deeply within his body that he now stands separate from ordinary men, just as you do, daughter of my pride and triumph, from ordinary women. Go forward, then, through the world, most precious to each other and terrifying to everyone else!"

"My father," Beatrice said weakly, and as she spoke she continued to keep her hand pressed against her heart, "why did you bring this terrible fate upon your child?"

"Miserable!" exclaimed Rappaccini. "What do you mean, foolish girl? Do you think it's misery to be blessed with incredible gifts that no power or strength could help an enemy overcome—misery to be able to defeat the strongest with just a breath—misery to be as terrifying as you are beautiful? Would you have preferred, then, the condition of a weak woman, vulnerable to all evil and capable of none?"

"I wish I could have been loved instead of feared," whispered Beatrice as she collapsed to the ground. "But that doesn't matter now. I'm leaving, father, going to a place where the evil you've worked so hard to blend into my very essence will fade away like a dream—just like the scent of these toxic flowers that will no longer poison my breath among the blossoms of Eden. Goodbye, Giovanni! Your hateful words feel like lead weighing down my heart, but even they will drop away as I rise up. Oh, wasn't there more poison in your soul than in mine from the very beginning?"

To Beatrice—whose earthly body had been so drastically transformed by Rappaccini's expertise—poison had become life itself, so the powerful antidote brought death; and thus the unfortunate victim of human cleverness and disrupted nature, and of the inevitable doom that follows all such attempts at twisted wisdom, died there at the feet of her father and Giovanni. At that very moment, Professor Pietro Baglioni appeared at the window and shouted loudly, his voice carrying both triumph and horror as he addressed the stunned man of science, "Rappaccini! Rappaccini! Is this what your experiment has accomplished!"

THE END

Thank You For Reading

You've Just Read a Piece of the Greatest Library Ever Rebuilt

Thank you for reading.

This book is one of thousands we're restoring, reimagining, and translating as part of the **Modern Library of Alexandria** — a global movement to preserve and share humanity's most important ideas.

What was once lost to fire and time is now rising again — not just as memory, but as living, breathing knowledge, freely accessible to all.

What You Can Do Next:

- **Keep Reading.**

  Discover more legendary works — in beautiful print, audiobook, or digital form — at LibraryofAlexandria.com.

- **Build Your Own Library.**

  Every title is available as a paperback, hardcover, or collectible boxset — at true printing cost. Craft a personal library worthy of display.

- **Spread the Light.**

  Share this book. Tell others about the movement. Help us translate every timeless work into every language, so no reader is ever left behind.

By finishing this book, you've already taken part in something extraordinary.

Join us at LibraryofAlexandria.com

Together, we're rebuilding the greatest library the world has ever known.

With appreciation,

The Modern Library of Alexandria Team

Visit:
www.libraryofalexandria.com
Or scan the code below: